Delta Public Library

D0843328

J629.13
SMI
AR:3.8
Pts:0.5

WITHDRAWN

DEC 4 2014

Machines at the Airport

Siân Smith

Heinemann LIBRARY

Chicago, Illinois

© 2014 Heinemann Library
an imprint of Capstone Global Library, LLC
Chicago, Illinois

All rights reserved. No part of this publication may be
reproduced or transmitted in any form or by any means,
electronic or mechanical, including photocopying.

Edited by Dan Nunn and John-Paul Wilkins
Designed by Cynthia Akiyoshi
Picture research by Elizabeth Alexander
Production by Sophia Argyris
Originated by Capstone Global Library Ltd
Printed and bound in China by Leo Paper Products Ltd

17 16 15 14 13
10 9 8 7 6 5 4 3 2 1

Library of Congress Cataloging-in-Publication Data
Cataloging-in-Publication data is available at the Library
of Congress: loc.gov

ISBN 978-1-4329-7499-2 (hardback)
ISBN 978-1-4329-7504-3 (paperback)

Acknowledgments
We would like to thank the following for permission to
reproduce photographs: Alamy pp. 4 (© Steve Vidler),
5 (© ITAR-TASS Photo Agency), 9 (© Kevpix), 12 (©
ROUSSEL BERNARD), 15 (© Tips Images / Tips Italia
Srl a socio unico), 18 (© imagebroker), 19 (© Richard
Wareham Fotografie), 22 (© Jim West); BULMOR
Airground Technologies GmbH p. 13; Corbis pp. 7 (©
Angelika Warmuth/dpa), 17 (© Patrice Latron); Getty
Images pp. 6, 8 (Baerbel Schmidt/Stone+), 10, 23
conveyor belt (Erik Dreyer/Stone); Shutterstock pp.
14, title page (© Robert Cumming), 16, 23 tug (©
Thomas Nord), 21, 23 pilot (© Andresr), 23 scanner (©
Voznikevich Konstantin), 23 fuel (© Concept Photo), 23
X-ray (© Kasza), 23 radar (© Gertan), SuperStock pp. 11
(© imagebroker.net), 20 (© Ton Koene / age footstock).

Design element photographs of airplane (© oriontrail),
airport runway (© Cindy Hughes), car engine part (©
fuyu liu), and gear cog (© Leremy) reproduced with
permission of Shutterstock.

Front cover photograph of an airplane reproduced with
permission of Getty Images (Yuji Kotani/Taxi Japan).
Back cover photograph of an air traffic controller holding
light wands (© Andresr) and a tug (© Thomas Nord)
reproduced with permission of Shutterstock.

We would like to thank Dee Reid and Marla Conn for
their invaluable help in the preparation of this book.

Every effort has been made to contact copyright holders
of material reproduced in this book. Any omissions will
be rectified in subsequent printings if notice is given to
the publisher.

All the Internet addresses (URLs) given in this book were
valid at the time of going to press. However, due to the
dynamic nature of the Internet, some addresses may
have changed, or sites may have changed or ceased to
exist since publication. While the author and publisher
regret any inconvenience this may cause readers, no
responsibility for any such changes can be accepted by
either the author or the publisher.

Contents

Some words are shown in bold, **like this**. You can find out what they mean by looking in the glossary.

Why Do We Have Machines at an Airport?

People make machines to do different jobs.

An airplane is a machine that helps us to travel to places that are far away.

People go to airports so that they can travel on airplanes.

Some machines at airports help people to get their bags onto airplanes.

Can a Machine Spot Dangerous Things?

People are not allowed to take things onto airplanes that could hurt other people.

Metal detectors are machines that can tell if people are carrying guns, knives, or other metal objects.

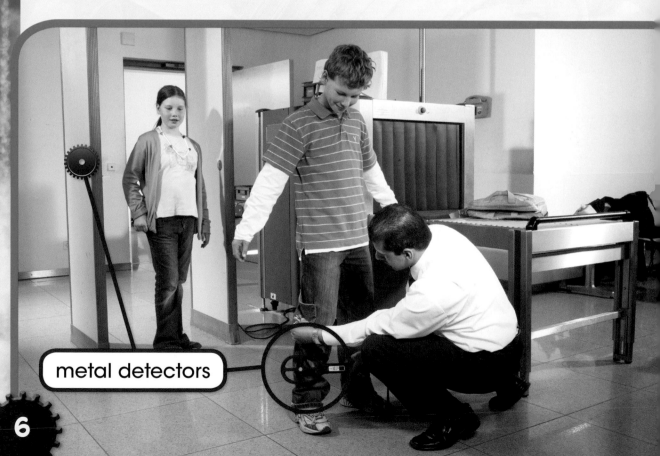

metal detectors

Some machines can take pictures of people that look a bit like an **X-ray**.

They can show if people have hidden things under their clothes.

Every bag at an airport has to go through an **X-ray** machine.

X-ray machines show pictures of things inside a bag, even when it is closed.

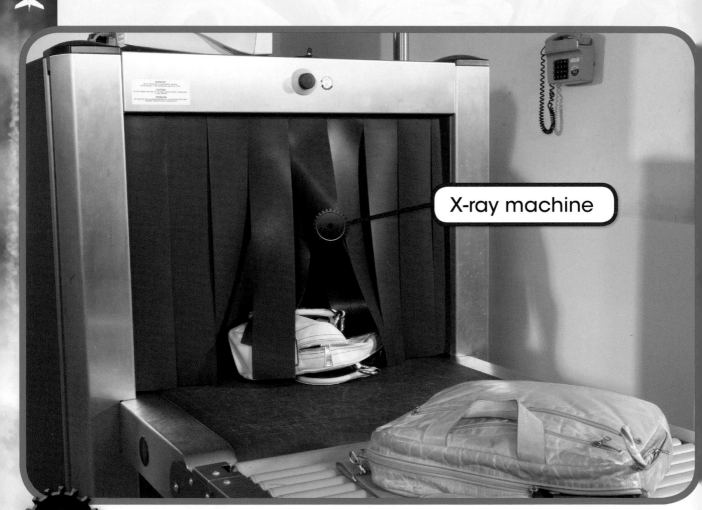

X-ray machine

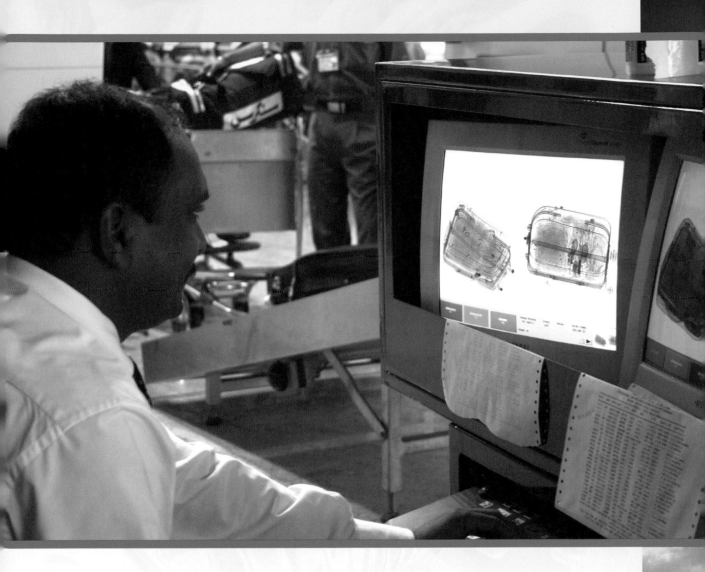

Different colors show what things are made of.

Airport workers check to see if the pictures show anything dangerous.

How Can Machines Help to Move Bags?

Each bag is given a number. Computers and **scanners** use the number to tell where each bag is and where it needs to go.

Moving belts called **conveyor belts** and carts carry the bags around.

conveyor belt

conveyor belt

belt loader

Sorting machines stop the bags from getting lost or stuck.

Special machines called belt loaders move bags onto the airplanes.

How Can Machines Help to Move People?

The doors on an airplane are high above the ground.

Sometimes a giant staircase on wheels helps people to get on and off an airplane.

ambulift

If people cannot walk, they can ride on special vehicles to move around an airport.

A machine called an ambulift can lift them up into an airplane.

What Are the Biggest Machines at an Airport?

The biggest machines at an airport are the airplanes.

Jet airplanes can carry hundreds of people.

Inside an airplane, there are many small machines that help the **pilot**.

Machines show the pilot how fast the plane is going, where the plane is, and how high it is in the air.

What Other Machines Help Airplanes?

Airplanes use their engines to move forward, but most cannot go backward.

An airplane tractor or **tug** moves an airplane to where it needs to be.

tug

refueler truck

hose

Airplanes are too big to go to gas stations, but they need **fuel** to make them move.

Refueler trucks with long hoses give airplanes the fuel they need.

Which Machines Help Airplanes in the Ice and Snow?

Airplanes need to go fast down a runway before they can take off into the air.

Snow plows push snow off runways so that planes can take off.

snow plow

runway

de-icer machine

Some parts of an airplane stop working if they are covered in ice.

De-icer machines lift airport workers up so they can spray special liquid to melt the ice.

What Stops Airplanes from Crashing into Each Other?

Airport workers guide planes around airports so that planes do not crash into each other.

Pictures from **radars** show them any planes in the sky and where they are going.

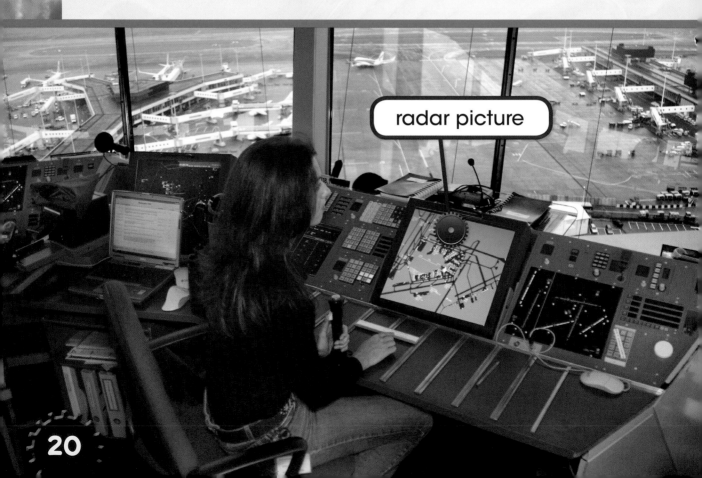

radar picture

light wand

Airport workers tell **pilots** when it is safe to land by using radios.

They also use light wands to tell pilots what to do when they are on the ground.

What Does This Machine Do?

Can you guess what this airport machine does?

Find the answer on page 24.

Picture Glossary

 **conveyor belt** moving belt that carries things along

 **scanner** machine that reads information from a label

 **fuel** liquid we put into airplanes to make them move

 **tug** type of tractor that pulls things along

 **pilot** driver of an airplane

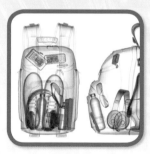 **X-ray** photo that shows the inside of something

 **radar** machine that can tell where airplanes are in the sky and which direction they are moving in

Find Out More

Books

Harrison, Sarah. *A Day at the Airport* (Time Goes By). Minneapolis: Millbrook, 2009.

Marsico, Katie. *Working at the Airport* (21st Century Junior Library: Careers). Ann Arbor: Cherry Lake, 2009.

Internet Sites

Facthound offers a safe, fun way to find Internet sites related to this book. All of the sites on Facthound have been researched by our staff.

Here's all you do:
Visit www.facthound.com
Type in this code:
9781432974992

Index

The airport machine on page 22 is a water truck. It collects waste from the toilets of the airplane.